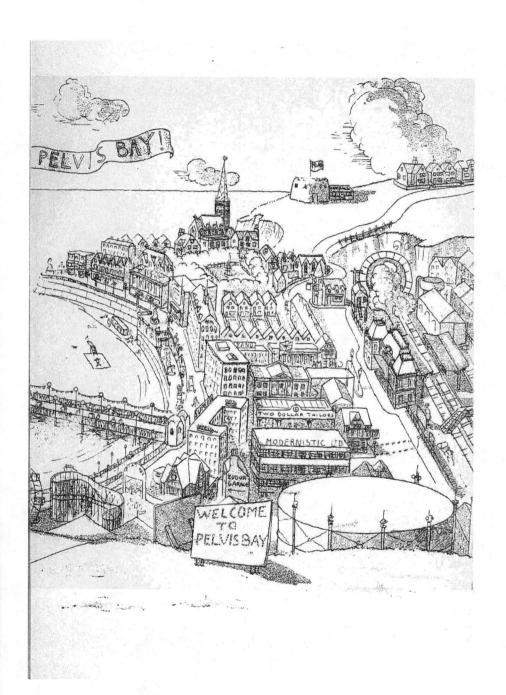

PROGRESS AT PELVIS BAY

BY

OSBERT LANCASTER

LONDON
JOHN MURRAY

Blocks of a few of the following illustrations by Mr. Lancaster have kindly been lent by the Architectural Review, in which Mr. Lancaster has already given some account of this well-known plague-spot and seaside eye-sore.

First Edition . . 1936
Reprinted November 1941
Reprinted . March 1944

PRINTED IN GREAT BRITAIN BY
JARROLD AND SONS LTD., NORWICH

FOREWORD

Of the Emperor Augustus it was said that he found Rome brick and left it marble, of the makers of modern Pelvis Bay it might well be said that they found it weather-boarding and left it chromium-plate. *Progress at Pelvis Bay* is a detailed account of a splendid metamorphosis. It traces with loving enthusiasm the development of a flourishing seaside resort from the original poverty-stricken fishing village to the present magnificent marine metropolis covering many acres of what had heretofore been virgin downland. By means of the numerous carefully chosen illustrations the reader is enabled to follow the various architectural changes that have taken place and to realize with what diligence the authorities have always striven to avail themselves of all that was Best in contemporary Art. The author can only hope that this modest epic of enlightened municipal development will inspire others to do likewise, and that through the length and breadth of England's green and pleasant land the numberless rapidly growing urban communities will similarly bear in mind that Taste should never be neglected in the interests of Commerce and Industry and that the path that lies before them is ever onward and upward with the Arts.

CONTENTS

A Brief History of the Town

WHILE Pelvis Bay, like most of our great seaside resorts, is largely the product of the nineteenth century, its healthy breezes and magnificent situation were appreciated by people of culture and discernment at a time when the larger part of this island was still in a state of the most primitive barbarism. Although no reference to its existence at this time has as yet come to light, the well-preserved remains of a Roman villa at Pelvis Magna (Open to the public on weekdays from May to September, entrance fee, 6d. Key at custodian's cottage) proves conclusively that its beauties were not unappreciated by the most luxurious nation of antiquity. Moreover, a very ancient local tradition holds that it was at Pelvis Bay, at a spot where the *Pair of Compasses* public-house now stands, that the Emperor Maximentius landed in A.D. 389. A fine mosaic pavement recently uncovered at the villa, showing a bearded man wading through what appears to be water, is taken by some to be a striking confirmation of this piece of folklore. However, another school holds that it is of much later date and in some way connected with fertility rites, a theory difficult to substantiate as unfortunately most of the central portion of the figure is missing.

With the departure of the legions Pelvis Bay lapsed into

I

1790

an obscurity from which it did not emerge until the dawn of the nineteenth century. Throughout the Middle Ages it was the home of a few poor fisherfolk with whose humble lives history has not concerned itself. In the late fourteenth century the manor of Pelvis, or Pylvis, came into the possession of the Champignon family, several of whose tombs are still visible in the parish church of St. Pancras (Late Norman, restored 1872).

It is at this period that we first find written references to the town under its present name of Pelvis, the exact etymology of which is obscure but is generally thought to have some reference to the formation of the local coast-line. (See Prof. Betjemans article, "Some anatomical place-names in Southern England," *Philological Quarterly*, June, 1905.)

2

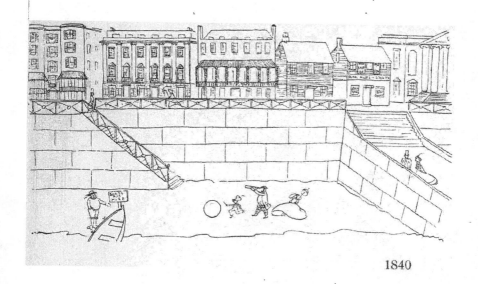

1840

From this date until the close of the eighteenth century the history of this little fishing village is almost devoid of incident. For some inexplicable reason it failed to contribute as much as a fishing smack to the fleet which defeated the Armada, but we can be certain that there were many gallant Pelvis lads who were present on that glorious occasion. In 1732 the Hereditary Prince of Sonderburg-Hildburghausen was driven ashore at Pelvis Bay by the great storm of November 17th while on his way from Danzig to Corunna.

This historic event was commemorated by a column erected on the west cliff (no longer standing). Little worthy of such commemoration as this incident may seem, it nevertheless had important consequences for the future of the town. Fifty years later his daughter, the Freifrau

3

1890

von Schwenkendorp, the last surviving lady-in-waiting to Queen Caroline, while staying in the neighbourhood had the curiosity to visit the spot where her father had first set foot on English soil. So charmed was she with the picturesque appearance of the little town that she forthwith decided to establish herself there in order to undergo the course of sea-bathing which she had been ordered by her doctors. Others soon followed her example, and by the beginning of the new century Pelvis Bay could boast a regular summer season.

It is matter for hearty congratulation that the town

1930

should have been discovered and launched by a woman of such high moral character as the Countess, as otherwise it might so easily have acquired the unsavoury reputation of contemporary Brighton ; a reputation which it would have found difficult to have lived down.

In 1810 it was decided, in order to check the erosion of the sea, to erect a sea-wall which proved the origin of the present promenade. Soon numerous rows of lodging houses sprang up and a number of private houses were erected, all, alas, in the monotonous style of the Regency. By the time Queen Victoria was on the throne the town could boast two churches, a chapel and several public

5

buildings of which some account will be given later. With the coming of the railway in the late 'fifties a new period of expansion commences, and from now until the Jubilee each year saw some notable addition to the town's amenities. In 1860 the promenade was enlarged. In '64 the foundation-stone of St. James-the-Least was laid. In '75 the new pier was opened, replacing the old jetty that had been destroyed in a gale some years previously. In the 'eighties the Ship Hotel, the band-stand and finally the beautiful Jubilee Memorial statue of the Queen followed one another in quick succession. The years that followed were ones of steady progress.

Came the War. The town was fortunate enough to escape the horrors of an enemy bombardment, and although no effort was spared towards " doing its bit," enjoyed a period of increased prosperity. The Allied Victory was commemorated by the laying out of the new public gardens on the lower promenade and the erection of a fine war memorial of which a more detailed appreciation will later be found.

In 1925 Pelvis Bay became a municipal borough, and a new period of building activity commenced. The Winter Garden was erected in a modified Renaissance style ; a palatial cinema made its appearance on the site of the last of the old Regency houses, and the great modern store near by was opened. Great care was taken by the Council that all these buildings should harmonize, and it was decided that they should all conform to the modified Renaissance of the Winter Garden. At the same time it was decided to recondition the pier, and at the suggestion of one of the councillors who had recently visited the

Colonial Exhibition in Paris, it was built in the Moorish style with the most gratifying results ; the two kiosks at the entrance blending very happily with the neo-Egyptian façade of the Hotel Splendide opposite. Finally, last year, the vast new bathing-pool, constructed on the site of the old Assembly Rooms, an uninteresting and inconvenient group of buildings dating from the late eighteenth century, was opened by the Mayor and the Pelvis Bay Carnival Queen, a Miss Withers of Tulse Hill, who went down the chute together in the presence of the Lord-Lieutenant and a distinguished gathering.

The Manor of Pelvis

OF the first manor house on this site, built at some time towards the end of the sixteenth century by Sir Guy Cinqbois who had married the last of the Champignons whose dowry it was, no trace remains. Moreover, alas, it has been found quite impossible to trace any picture or print to give us some idea of its appearance. However, one is perhaps justified in picturing to oneself some quaint, half-timbered old place, covered with roses and surrounded by old-world gardens. Alas, if ever these imaginary delights actually existed, it is obvious that they had but little appeal for Sir Guy's grandson, Sir Ralph, who, early in the eighteenth century, pulled down the old homestead and erected in its place a gaunt and foreign-looking mansion for whose destruction numerous contemporary prints and pictures forbid us to weep. Later in the century his son and successor laid out the park in the ludicrous contemporary style introduced by " Capability " Brown. With the succession to the title of Sir Ossian in 1805, the old place recaptured some of its pristine picturesqueness. With the assistance of the talented Mr. Wyattville he rapidly converted the dreary eighteenth-century barrack into a romantic medieval structure more in keeping with the dignity of his family and the antiquity of the site. Not

9

B

1750

only was the skyline adorned with castellations and the
old-fashioned windows given a Gothic air, but a magnificent watch-tower was also added, from the top of
which a glorious view of seven counties was obtainable.
Admirable as these improvements undoubtedly were, they
were not, nor could be at that early date when our knowledge of architecture had not yet reached perfection,
quite *true*. So that when, in 1875, Sir Arthur Cinqbois
decided to rebuild, while many regretted the old castle,
it was fully realized that owing to the enormously increased
sum of architectural knowledge, the new building would
undoubtedly be a great improvement on the old. And
so indeed it proved. Sir Arthur, after much thought, had
come to the wise decision that the most suitable style to
employ would be the Jacobean, a decision that won
universal approval. When it was finished, Pelvis Towers,

1810

as it was now called, though not perhaps so large as
Compton Wynyates, and lacking the historical associations
of Hatfield, was certainly to be reckoned among the state-
liest of English homes. The rich colour of the brick, the
delicate quality of the terra-cotta enrichments, the charming fantasy of such details as the chimneys, all combined
to make an unforgettable impression on every visitor.

On the death of Sir Arthur, his trustees in bankruptcy
(since the failure of the old gentleman's frequent gallant
attempts to win the Derby he had tended to divide most
of his time between Homburg and Monte Carlo) disposed

11

1875

of the estate to Mordecai Finkelstein, that far-sighted Im-
perialist from South Africa, who added a new wing in the
Tudor style for the accommodation of King Edward VII,
then Prince of Wales, when he spent a week-end at Pelvis
Towers in the late 'nineties. Soon after this Mr. Finkelstein's great services to the Empire were rewarded with
a baronetcy, and on marrying the late Sir Arthur's youngest
daughter in the same year he changed his name by deed-
poll to Cinqbois, thus insuring the continuity of that
illustrious family.

During the war, Sir Mordecai very gallantly put his
historic mansion at the disposal of his country and it
became for four years a convalescent home for wounded
officers. After the war Sir Mordecai's son, Sir Angus,

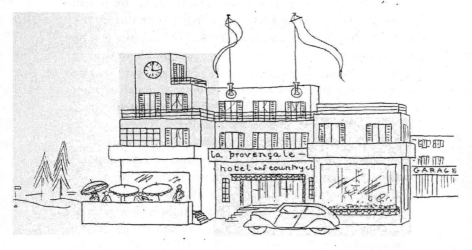

1932

resided at Pelvis Towers until 1929 when an adverse decision arrived at in a complicated legal dispute arising out of the affairs of Consolidated Finkelstein Developments Ltd. made it seem unlikely that Sir Angus would be able to spend much of his time at his old home for the following fourteen years and he decided, after considerable mental anguish, to part with it.

In 1930 the estate was acquired by the Pelvis Bay Country Club Ltd., a company formed in order to modernize the old house and to run it as an exclusive country club. The plans for the new clubhouse were the work of the distinguished continental architect, Hans Krautenbaum, whom the political events in his own country had forced to eat the bread of exile in a foreign land. His original plans were thought by the District Council, and other

13

authorities to whom they were submitted, to be a trifle too daring in conception, and although doubtless they would have been quite suitable for the continent they would hardly, it was thought, prove acceptable to the type of visitor it was hoped to attract. So they were in some slight degree modified by a distinguished local architect with the happiest results. While it is undoubtedly tragic to think of fine old houses such as Pelvis Towers passing out of the hands of those who have owned them for countless generations, the necessity for progress and development cannot be denied, and although there were many who regretted the passing of the old ivy-covered walls and quaint mullions of the seat of the Cinqbois, few who are acquainted with the cocktail-bar, the squash courts, the eighteen-hole golf-course and other delights of " La Provençale," as the clubhouse is now called, will be found to admit that the change is altogether for the worse.

Accommodation

THE evolution of the great modern luxury hotel from its humble beginnings as a wayside inn is one of the most fascinating phenomena of recent times and nowhere can it be studied to greater advantage than at Pelvis Bay. By the courtesy of the proprietors of the Ship Hotel, I am able to publish a remarkable series of pictures which show in the clearest possible way, and in considerable detail, the various stages through which this historic hostelry has passed. When Pelvis Bay was still a poverty-stricken collection of fishermen's huts it could only boast one tavern, the Ship, a wretched weather-boarded cottage on the quay. While this doubtless proved quite adequate for the needs of the simple fisherfolk it was in no way capable of satisfying the more exigeant requirements of the summer visitors. However, as at first the majority of these preferred to rent apartments rather than to stay in an hotel, and as the proprietor of the inn lacked both the capital and the initiative to expand, it was not until the house had been acquired by a syndicate at the time of the coming of the railway that it was decided to rebuild.

Once this decision had been arrived at the work was immediately put into the best possible hands ; namely,

1870

those of Sir Septimus Ogive. He was given carte blanche
and assured that no expense would be spared to make
this the finest hotel in Europe and an example of what
a great modern hotel could and should be. The style
decided upon was thirteenth-century Flemish-East Anglian
and this was rigidly kept to throughout, even such small
details as the fire-screens and the gasoliers being personally
designed by the architect.

The result was almost miraculous and immediately
evoked the most widespread admiration. In fact it was
confidently stated by contemporary critics that for purity
of design there were only three buildings of the same
period in the country that could even approach it; the
Randolph Hotel at Oxford, the Angel Choir at Lincoln and

16

1902

the St. Pancras Railway Station. Many famous figures
of the Victorian Age were at one time or another visitors
to this hotel, and many of them have left eloquent tokens
of their appreciation in the historic visitors' book. Thus
we find after Mr. Ruskin's name the following beautiful
compliment : " Not only is the water hot but the bathroom has a Moral Beauty of its own in no way connected
with its mere utilitarian value." Two or three pages
later we find Alfred (not then Lord) Tennyson starting a
complaint as to the condition in which his shirts have
returned from the laundry with the witty comment,
" Tears, idle tears, I know not what they mean ! " In
the manager's office is still preserved a letter from Dickens
pointing out that the boot-boy had gone off with his

17

1922

trousers, a laughable incident that the great man himself
was the first to appreciate.

However, despite a natural reluctance on the part of
the management to change these almost hallowed surroundings it was decided at the time of the accession of
King Edward VII, much to the understandable annoyance
of Sir Septimus, that the time had come to redecorate the
hotel throughout and to adopt various modern improvements. While the interior was completely renovated, the
greatest care was taken that the celebrated façade should
in no way be altered. Electric lighting, a passenger lift
and numerous additional bathrooms were installed, and
all the public rooms were done up in the style of Louis-
Seize. The effect was, at the time, generally admired,

1930

recalling, as a contemporary newspaper happily phrased it, " memories of the gracious days of the *ancien régime*, when powdered *beaux* paid their court to the beauties of Versailles in the fairy-like surroundings of the -Petit Trianon."

In architectural circles the liveliest satisfaction was felt by all, that the management had had no truck with the Art Nouveau Movement, then at the height of its short-lived popularity.

This scheme of decoration remained unchanged until after the war, when it was felt that perhaps the time had come to make a change. The stately and slightly austere character of the Edwardian *décor* was considered to be rather out of keeping with the increased tempo of the machine age, and so it was decided to convert the interior into an old-world Tudor Hall. This, of course, involved extensive structural alterations of which the most important was the removal of the twin Corinthian pillars in the entrance hall and the subsequent underpinning of the roof. So skilfully was this carried out and so great was the care taken to ensure that no modern feature should occur to interfere with the illusion of antiquity, that few visitors to the hotel were ever remotely aware that the age-old oak beams above their heads were in reality solid pressed steel carefully grained and varnished !

So great, however, is the pace of modern life that in a very few years the management, in pursuance of their well-known policy of always keeping abreast of the times, determined once more to redecorate their premises. In 1929, when so much alteration and rebuilding were going on all over the town, they built the new Chinese Grill Room on the front and the following year called in a well-known firm of Mayfair decorators to transform the rest of the hotel.

The keynote of the scheme of decoration adopted was that of a ship, and every effort was made to emphasize this nautical idea in all the details of the furnishing, with such successful results that the illusion of being on ship-board is almost complete and is only slightly impaired by the uninterrupted view of the sea obtainable from most of the windows ; were it invisible there would be nothing to indicate that one was not on the most modern of trans-atlantic liners.

As a Shopping Centre

PELVIS BAY has always been justly proud of its many
magnificent shops, and the city fathers have always
considered it their duty to do all that lay in their power
to assist the local shop-keeping community.

One of the most difficult problems with which town
councils and other local authorities are confronted to-day
is that connected with the preservation of old buildings
in general and shop-fronts in particular. How best to
satisfy the conflicting claims of modern business efficiency,
and reverence for, and appreciation of, picturesque
antiquity. Happily in Pelvis Bay the question hardly
arises, for, with the exception of " Ye Olde Toffee Shoppe "
on the parade, the town can boast of few really old, that
is to say Tudor, shop-fronts, and when private enterprise
decides on modernizing the existing nineteenth-century
façades the authorities render them every possible encouragement. It is with the greatest pleasure that I find
myself in a position, through the kindness of the proprietors, to publish a series of pictures illustrating the
various changes through which one of the best-known
establishments in the town, Messrs. Wallop, the drapers
on the corner of the Marine Parade, have passed since
their foundation, nearly one hundred years ago.

The original shop founded by the first Wallop was a poky little affair with windows of indifferent glass and lit by oil lamps which, in the winter, remained lit all day, so dark was the interior, and, according to the fast-diminishing band of those who have any personal recollection of it, it was not generally regretted when the time came to rebuild. The new shop when it opened in the late 'seventies was universally admitted to be a great improvement on the old. At that time it was considered the very last word in modern shop-fronts and it was not

22

until some years after the war, when a great expansion
of business made it necessary, that there was any thought
on the part of Mr. Wallop of abandoning the premises.
After due consideration it was decided that rather than
move from the excellent site that the firm had occupied
for so long on the corner of the Marine Parade and the
High Street it would be far better to acquire the adjoining
premises and rebuild. When this decision first became

known there were not a few hearts in Pelvis Bay that missed a beat, so familiar and so lovable, if I may use the phrase in this connection, had the old shop-front become.

Many there were who viewed the proposed changes with the gravest foreboding, feeling that what had been good enough for their parents should be good enough for the present generation, and, maybe, mistrusting the ability of the modern builder to supply a suitable and worthy substitute for the old Victorian façade.

To realize how groundless these fears proved, one has only to compare the illustrations above. On page 23 the old dingy front, the available window space stupidly broken up by iron columns, covered with polished brass the cleaning of which made serious inroads on the time of the employees, and overleaf the cheery new modernistic front. While feeling that the pictures are fully qualified

24

to speak for themselves, one would like to draw attention to the materials in which the new front is carried out. The surround is entirely in chromium plating, which, while it always looks bright and cheerful, has the great advantage of being able to achieve an effect of high polish without making any demands on " elbow-grease." The border is encrusted with a charming pomegranate design, while the lettering is chromium steel on a background of black glass. At night the whole is illuminated by horizontal bands of red and blue neon tubes.

At the same time as these premises were opened it

C

was decided to establish another branch of the shop farther up the High Street to cater for a slightly more exclusive public and to deal in a special line of artistic and hand-made goods that had hitherto been sold in the Artwear department. This was under the capable management of Miss Janet Wallop who had studied at the Slade school and had a wide knowledge of hand-weaving, peasant embroidery and kindred subjects. The decoration of this new shop was very different to that of the larger one on the corner, and was especially designed to emphasize the Artistic and non-commercial nature of the goods sold. It met at once with the greatest success, and now there is an almost continuous stream of both visitors and residents passing through the charming old-world doorway of this delightful shop that is " different."

Places of Worship

WHEN Pelvis Bay was still nothing but a collection of fishermen's huts, the nearest church was that of St. Pancras at Pelvis Magna, three miles inland. The simple devotion of the hardy fisherfolk made light of this six-mile tramp every Sunday, but it was not to be expected that the new annual visitors, many of whom were in delicate health, would not soon feel the want of some place of worship a little closer at hand. Moreover, its distance from the town was not the only disadvantage attaching to the old parish church ; for during the earlier part of the century the incumbent, the Rev. Augustus Cinqbois, Sir Ossian's brother, could not be said in any way to share in that quickening of the nation's religious life that was such a feature of the period. He was, perhaps, although fundamentally a most God-fearing man, rather too typical a product of the eighteenth century, and his habit of conducting the service in full hunting kit and his remarkable capacity for port did little to endear him to either Evangelicals or Tractarians. So it was decided to erect a church in the town itself and the work was entrusted to a prominent London architect, and the consecration took place in 1835. It was perhaps a little unfortunate that the church of St. Paul was built when it was, for,

THE CHURCH OF ST. PAUL

28

despite a great deal of local opposition and the spirited protests of the Camden Society, the style chosen was that degraded classical that was even then fast losing ground. As it was, the town had to wait another thirty years for a church that was acceptable to those who agreed with the present Bishop of London in thinking no church is a proper church " that has not a spire pointing a finger to God," as His Lordship so aptly puts it. Luckily St. Paul's is no longer standing to reproach the town with its former lack of taste as last year it was pulled down and the site disposed of by the Ecclesiastical Authorities to a prominent film combine who are this year opening a magnificent cinema, the Damascus, on the site.

The new church of St. James-the-Least, when it was finally opened in the late 'sixties, was universally admitted to have been well worth waiting for. Built in the Early Perpendicular style it also managed cleverly to incorporate several elements of both Flemish and Venetian Gothic of the best periods. The architect was Sir Septimus Ogive (a friend and pupil of the celebrated Sir Gilbert Scott) who was a resident of Pelvis Bay for many years and recently died there at the advanced age of a hundred and two, and is buried in the shadow of what is generally considered his masterpiece. This remarkable veteran was active and true to his principles to the end, and indeed his death was generally attributed to a fit of apoplexy caused by his justifiable annoyance at the incomprehensible rejection by the county council of his plans for an Early English airport. The spire of this remarkable church is one of the highest in the south of England and is a landmark for miles around and visible far out at sea. The interior

ST. JAMES-THE-LEAST

is no less remarkable, and no visitor to Pelvis Bay should fail to pay it a visit. Lack of space forbids me to enumerate the various artistic treasures it contains and I must content myself with drawing attention to some of the finest. The beautiful East Window in which the story of St. Philip and the Ethiopian eunuch is portrayed in glowing colours was put up in 1902 as a memorial to two members of the congregation who spent their lives in the mission field in Abyssinia. The beautiful marble font, decorated with the Passage over Jordan in bas-relief, the work of a well-known local sculptress, was the gift of Sir Mordecai Cinqbois (*né* Finkelstein) on his baptism. The lovely alabaster reredos, with a pattern of water-lilies in lapis-lazuli inlay, was given to the church in 1905 by an anonymous donor and is generally considered to be one of the masterpieces of *l'Art Nouveau* in this country. The encaustic tiles in the main aisle are another treasure that the visitor should be careful not to overlook, as in point of colour they are not surpassed, in Professor Betjeman's opinion, by any of this date in the whole of England.

However, the C. of E., though foremost, was not alone in providing the town with fine specimens of modern ecclesiastical architecture. The Baptists, the Methodists, both primitive and ordinary, the Seventh Day Adventists, the Plymouth Brethren and even the Irvingites have all at one time or another established places of worship in the town, of which the Strict Baptist chapel in the Station Road, a thirteenth-century Gothic building in Sussex Flint, is perhaps the most notable (see illustration). The R.C.'s have the church of St. Philip Neri, a building whose beauty of design renders the spectator almost oblivious

THE STRICT BAPTIST CHAPEL

to the somewhat harsh appearance of the corrugated iron
in which it is built. The most recent addition to this
list is perhaps also the finest, namely the one hundred
and twenty-second Church of Christ Scientist in Campbell-
Bannerman Terrace. It is a magnificent red-brick structure built in the Romanesque style to which many other
temples of this sect throughout the country have accustomed
us. It cost one hundred and twenty thousand pounds to
build, and the interior is adorned with a remarkable series
of mosaics depicting scenes from the life of Mrs. Eddy.

THE CHURCH OF CHRIST SCIENTIST

Monumental Art

WHILE a small town such as Pelvis Bay naturally cannot hope to compare with any of the larger or longer-established centres of population in the manner of public monuments, it does however possess a wealth of monumental art of which few towns of the same size can boast. It has been always a matter of considerable pride to the city fathers that no opportunity of commemorating either the illustrious dead or the many proud moments of our national history in which our town has had a share, however small, has ever been let slip.

The first monument ever to be erected in Pelvis Bay of which we have any record, was the Sonderburg-Hildburghausen Obelisk (see page 3) on the west cliff. Unfortunately owing to the insecurity of its foundations and the constant erosion of the sea this collapsed many years ago without leaving a trace behind. During the period immediately following the discovery of the town as a health resort those responsible for the development of Pelvis Bay were far too busy coping with the demand for increased accommodation to have either the time or capital to spare for non-utilitarian architecture. So it was not until the middle of the century that the first of the existing monuments was put up. This was the handsome

35

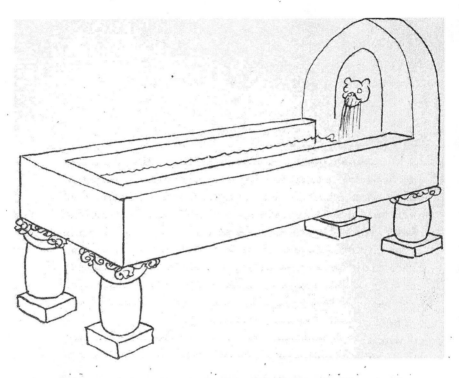

Gothic horse-trough that stands at the east end of the parade
where formerly the road went down to the beach; this
was the work of a well-known London architect, a pupil
of Pugin, and was erected at the expense of various ladies
resident in the town who had long noticed and pitied the
sad state of exhaustion to which the horses carting shingle
from the foreshore were reduced in the hot weather.
Next in date comes the superb Blenkinsop Memorial
Fountain in the public gardens which that great-hearted
benefactor of Pelvis Bay presented to the town in the

THE BLENKINSOP MEMORIAL

early 'seventies. This, an early work of Sir Septimus Ogive (see page 27), is remarkable both for the purity of the design and the richness of the decoration. The small thirteenth-century shrine which encloses the bust of the deceased is a veritable miracle of workmanship and the skill with which the architect has treated the terminal lantern affords a most striking demonstration of his wonderful ability to combine the Useful and the Ornamental.

The Jubilee of 1887 is commemorated by the fine statue of the Queen at the west end of the Promenade, a product of Miss Spiking's clever chisel (see below). Ten years later the Diamond Jubilee was marked by the erection of the fine new public lavatories to the east of the pier. A little farther along the Marine Parade we come to the dignified statue of the late General Sir Almeric Baffle, K.C.B., K.C.M.G., C.S.I., etc. The General, who was one of Pelvis Bay's most distinguished sons, was born at Pelvis St. Swithin, four miles inland, in 1813, and died at " Chillianwallah," Marine Parade, 1917. In the course of his long and gallant career in the Army he had served, with invariable distinction, in the fourth, fifth and ninth Zulu Wars, in the eleventh and twelfth Sikh Wars and in the Rangoon River Campaign of '56. It was in the fifth Zulu War that he won for himself not only the Victoria Cross but also the proud title of the Hero of Zimbabwe. During the Boer War he was in command of the Coastal Defence in the north of England and in 1914, although then in his hundredth year, he heard once more his country's call and emerged from his retirement to place his services at the disposal of the War Office,

IN ⚔ MEMORY
OF MAJ GENERAL
SIR ALPIERIG BAFFLE
KCB. KCVO. KCMC.
"HERO OF ZIMBABWE"
BORN MCMXVIII
DIED MCMXLIX. RIP

who promptly nominated him to a high administrative post in the Air Force, which he held until his death.

The Great War, which gave the gallant general the opportunity, for which he had always longed, to die in harness, is commemorated by a beautiful group of statuary on the lower promenade. It is in bronze and depicts the goddess of Victory in the act of crowning one of our gallant seamen with a laurel wreath. Although Pelvis Bay has long since ceased to have any direct connection with the Royal Navy, it was felt, in view of the town's glorious traditions, that a " Jack Tar " would be more suitable than the customary " Tommy." The whole group is the work of a well-known local sculptress, Miss Beatrice Spiking, who has been exhibiting regularly at the Royal Academy since the 'eighties. It was she who was responsible for the statue of Queen Victoria put up in '88, and it is hoped that she will be able to undertake the statue of the late King which it has been decided to erect this year. If she does, we feel that this will indeed constitute a record !

Other monuments, which, although we have been unable through lack of space to include illustrations of them, are well worth the visitor's attention, are the Boer War Memorial on the upper promenade, the charming bird-bath outside the Town Hall erected in memory of all those dumb animals who laid down their lives in the late war and the Wellington column in the Station Road that marks the spot where the Iron Duke once alighted from the train, by mistake as it was subsequently discovered.

D

Domestic Architecture and Housing

IT is obvious that in the realm of domestic architecture, the municipality has little opportunity or indeed right, to exercise any very direct influence. Moreover, the authorities at Pelvis Bay have never had any sympathy with town-planning or any such Socialist nonsense, preferring rather to leave things to the natural good taste of the individual. Their policy, it will, I fancy, be conceded by all unbiased observers, has been abundantly justified. In the following illustrations the uniformly high standard of building, more particularly in the modern examples, is very noticeable.

Like most seaside towns that developed rapidly at the beginning of the last century, Pelvis Bay has, or rather had, numerous terraces of houses, built in a uniformly monotonous style, of which Coburg Terrace, illustrated below, is a typical example. Happily the majority of them have been pulled down within the last few years, and at the moment Coburg Terrace itself is scheduled for demolition in the near future. A row of fine new shops will be erected on the site, the most notable of which will be Maisie's Café, the proprietors of this popular rendezvous having found their present premises in the High Street quite inadequate, and by next summer it is hoped that

43

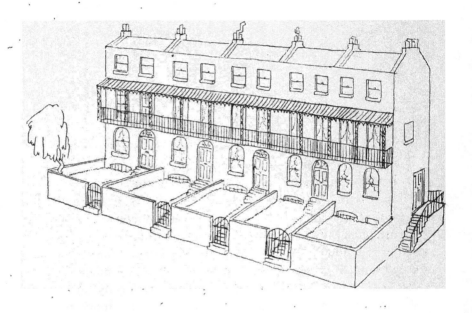

their magnificent new establishment will be opened on
this site. The plans and elevations are already complete
and on exhibition and should go far towards allaying the
apprehensions of those whose first reaction on hearing of
the erection of a new building in place of an old is one
of alarm. They show a charming two-storied building
in the Tudor style, with an old English roof-garden, and
will undoubtedly prove a notable addition to the already
long list of representative specimens of modern architecture
on the promenade.

In these circumstances, to regret the passing of the dingy
old row of houses, is to lay oneself open to the charge of
odious sentimentality.

44

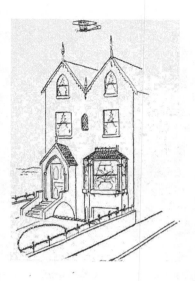

Rather later in date than Coburg Terrace is "Balmoral," two blocks farther along the front. Erected in the middle of the last century, this charming building has been ever since a high-class private hotel. Though nowadays it may appear, perhaps, a trifle old-fashioned to some people, the façade has a distinct character of its own. The interior, while retaining all its old-world dignity and restraint as regards decoration, was modernized shortly before the war when a bathroom and gas-lighting were installed. Among its faithful clientele are many who have come year after year since the hotel first opened its doors.

It is the presence in the town of numerous old-fashioned establishments of this type that gives to Pelvis Bay its unique atmosphere of respectability in the midst of progress. Long may they flourish!

Of a slightly different type, though almost contemporary, is "Osborne." This dignified and comfortable old house is one of those erected on what were then the outskirts of the town when Pelvis Bay first became popular as a place of retirement for the military and professional classes. A great feature of these houses are the large park-like gardens and impressive entrance gates. The ideal of those who developed this section of the town, and one which it must be admitted was faithfully realized, was " rus in urbe." This particular house was for long the residence of Admiral Sir Carraway Hawksmoor, afterwards first Viscount Honduras.

However comfortable and pleasing as many of these houses are, they have only to be compared to some of the modern labour-saving villas put up since the war in order to realize what enormous strides domestic architecture has made in recent years.

These charming houses, of which " Craigweil," the residence of the Mayor, Councillor Busfun, illustrated above, is a typical example, are not only magnificently planned and fitted with every modern labour-saving device, but are also possessed of those qualities of quaintness and cosiness which are so notably absent from some of the more recent examples of the so-called " modern " architecture. Moreover, they have been especially designed to harmonize with the beautiful landscape of the downs on which they have recently been erected in large numbers ; for despite its willingness to give every encouragement to justifiable commercial enterprise, the Council is never forgetful of its duties as a custodian of rural amenities.

The best example of this praiseworthy anxiety on the part of the council for the preservation of that rustic beauty

47

with which the immediate neighbourhood of Pelvis Bay is so singularly blessed, is perhaps to be found in the new housing estate on the west cliff. Here the greatest care has been taken to avoid all suspicion of urban monotony and the utmost variety of architecture has therefore been encouraged. Belvedere Avenue, the street illustrated above, was one of the first to be completed, and already well over half the houses are occupied. A striking tribute to the council's policy of insisting on the erection of dwellings with an individual character of their own and turning a deaf ear to all those cranks and so-called Modernists who are so constantly urging the merits of vast stream-lined, undecorated blocks of flats or rather tenements ; despite the fact that they are likely to have little appeal to a people whose proud boast it is that "An Englishman's Home is his Castle." Do they realize, one wonders, when they try to foist these continental barracks on us, that English is the only language that has a word for "home"?

Public Buildings

THE fact that a town is most often judged by the number and dignity of its public buildings is one that the makers of Pelvis Bay have always borne in mind. In the original fishing village there was, of course, no need for any town hall or other administrative centre ; what few public discussions took place were carried on either in the inn or the church porch, but when the town found itself expanding at a rapid rate the need for some sort of municipal offices became pressing.

The first town hall was erected in the 'forties and was a depressing stucco building with a pompous Doric portico, now happily no more, occupying the site of the Hotel Splendide. It was pulled down in the 'eighties and the present dignified edifice in the High Street took its place, the cheerful red-brick and terra-cotta of the façade forming a welcome contrast to the dingy stucco of its predecessor.

When the railway first came to Pelvis Bay, and for many years afterwards, the railway station was a mere shed that served well enough to shelter the passengers from the rain, but had no claim at all to any architectural merits. In the late 'seventies it was decided that this state of affairs had lasted quite long enough and the time had come for the provision of a more dignified entrance

to what was by this time one of Britain's premier seaside
resorts. In 1878 the new station was completed and
declared open by the Lord-Lieutenant in the presence of
the board of directors of the railway and a distinguished
gathering. It was a fine yellow brick building with stone
facings in the French Renaissance style and has since
become familiar to many thousands of annual visitors.

A noteworthy feature, and one that was considered to be something in the nature of a novelty at the time, was the Refreshment Buffet, and many men and women who now are grandparents retain the liveliest recollections of its delicious bath buns and tasty sandwiches, which remain to-day quite unchanged since the days of their youth.

Some years previous to the coming of the railway the Theatre Royal had first opened its doors, and it forthwith enjoyed many successful summer seasons until it was burnt down in the early 'seventies and subsequently replaced by the present building where regular seasons of Gilbert and Sullivan and other modern plays draw large houses throughout the summer. However, a new and better theatre was not the only result of this disastrous conflagration ; it drew the attention of the town authorities to the inadequate nature of the available fire-fighting apparatus and determined them to build and equip the present

53

magnificent fire station. It is a fine red-brick building
in the Romanesque style, the work of Sir Septimus Ogive,
and has accommodation for three fire engines with the
usual complement of escapes, hoses, firemen, etc.

Among the more recent additions to the list of public buildings that adorn Pelvis Bay are the Tramway depot and the Cottage Hospital. The former is a very striking erection on the Pelvis Magna Road, the work of one of our younger architects, and while some of the more old-fashioned of us may feel a little startled at first by its uncompromising modernity, it will be generally admitted that besides admirably fulfilling its function as a depot for trams it has also a stern machine-made beauty of its own.

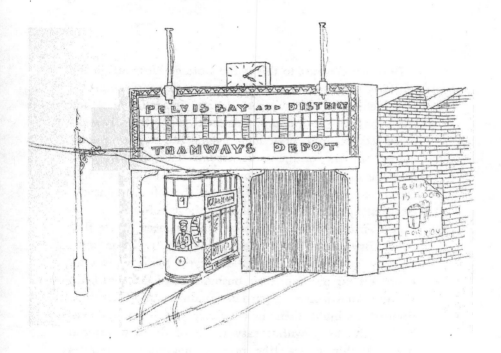

In direct contrast to this is the Cottage Hospital on the
outskirts of the town, a building of such convincing old-
world charm that many people are amazed when they
learn that it is not, as they imagined, a particularly well-
preserved example of a late seventeenth-century manor
house, but one of the most modern and best-equipped
hospitals of its size in the county and moreover was only
completed last year. The wing on the left contains the
electricity plant, that on the right the laboratory.

Few visitors to the town have hitherto been aware that
Pelvis Bay could boast many manufactures, nor until
recently could it. In 1928, however, following on an
enormous expansion of their business, Lead Gnomes Ltd.,
the well-known firm of garden ornament manufacturers,
decided to build their new factory out on the downs
behind the town within easy reach of the new arterial
road. Within a year the present magnificent premises
were complete and they provided a splendid object-lesson

56

to those who imagine that a factory must of necessity be an eyesore. One would never dream, on first catching sight of this fine pile that behind the handsome neo-Egyptian façade, with its lotus pillars and decorations of coloured tiles, is the most up-to-date plant of its kind in the world, throbbing away constantly with a daily output of over four hundred lead gnomes, bird-baths and Japanese storks.

A mile or so away, on the other side of the downs, stand the Municipal Waterworks. These are not usually a welcome addition to a rural landscape and when the Borough Council were recently faced with the problem of their erection, every care was taken that they should blend unobtrusively with the surrounding countryside. The result of their praiseworthy efforts towards the preservation of amenities is, as a recent visitor so happily phrased it, that unless one is near enough to hear the pumping, one would imagine that one was face to face with an old-world barn alongside a giant dovecote.

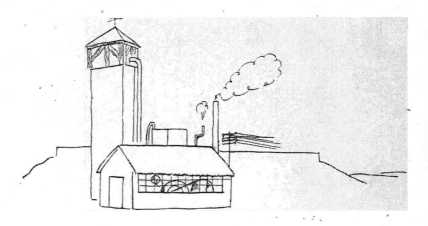

Methods of Transport

IT was thought that the following pictures of the various types of public conveyance that have at different times operated in the vicinity of Pelvis Bay, drawn from contemporary sources, might possibly be of some interest to the modern reader and serve to illustrate the development of local transport.

The first shows an old-fashioned waggonette or char-à-banc that used to run in the summer between Pelvis Bay

and various beauty-spots in the neighbourhood. It

started from Smith's Stables in the High Street, and the fare for the round trip, Pelvis Magna, Porkthorpe Castle, Wetstairs and back was half a crown a head.

Next comes the first motor vehicle (a two-cylinder, chain-driven De Dion-Panhard) ever to ply for hire in Pelvis Bay. It was put on the road by the enterprising

Mr. Smith in the summer of 1908 and made several successful trips along the coast until it finally exploded on the hill going up to Pelvis Magna one hot afternoon in the summer of 1909—a laughable incident that was fortunately attended by small loss of life and caused considerable pleasure to several of the more old-fashioned residents.

Thus Pelvis Bay, ever progressive, can justly claim to be the scene of the first serious char-à-banc disaster that ever occurred in this country !

It is a far cry from that ill-fated machine to this typical specimen of the splendid modern fleet of motor-buses and

char-à-bancs that offer such numerous opportunities for comfortable sight-seeing to the present-day visitor to the town. At the height of the season as many as fifty or sixty of these luxury coaches leave daily from the square opposite the town hall and almost as many bring visitors into the town from London and various neighbouring resorts.

Last summer, for the first time, an air service was operated to Pelvis Bay and at the wonderful new airport only six miles outside the town, not only can one avail oneself of the direct service to the capital and various other parts of the country, but also for the modest sum of five shillings one can enjoy a " round the town flight " in a luxurious new air-liner ; an experience that gives one quite a new

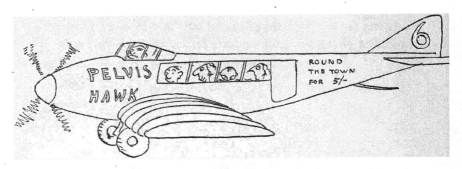

idea of the beauties of Pelvis Bay and the surrounding country.

The Journey Back

MANY of the thousands who, during the summer, motor down to Pelvis Bay by way of the new Flushbrook By-pass, must be familiar with the castellated tower of the " Hearts Are Trumps " roadhouse, but few, we suspect, are acquainted with the interesting history of the old place.

It seems probable that a farm-house of some description had existed on this site for several hundred years and had, moreover, remained in the hands of one family, the Blood-worthys, for a large proportion of that time. The oldest portion of the present structure, however, goes back no further than the late eighteenth century.

In those far-off days there was little or no traffic, the road indeed being little better than a winding cart-track, and so there was nothing for the Bloodworthys to do but farm their land ; but towards the end of the last century with the invention and speedy popularization of the bicycle there came a change.

The Widow Bloodworthy, her husband, a well-known and universally respected farmer, having died some years previously, found that she could make an acceptable addition to her income (she was the mother of seventeen children and farming was not what it was) by providing

1830

cyclists with tea and light refreshments. This soon became so profitable that she was enabled to invest in a rustic porch and some window-boxes, thus lending a picturesque air to the gaunt old farm-house, which provided an inspiration to many a contemporary water-colour painter. With the coming of the internal combustion engine early in the present century her profits from this source rapidly increased. Her humble establishment and its simple fare derived an added cachet at this time from the frequent stoppages in the neighbourhood of distinguished and often titled motorists, caused by the manifold imperfections of these early automobiles, on their way to week-end parties at Sir Mordecai Cinqbois at Pelvis Manor. On one occasion, indeed, she even sheltered Royalty under her roof, a glorious event the details of which she was never tired of recounting to her friends and visitors.

During the war, gallantly choosing as her motto " Business as Usual," she drove a thriving trade with the numerous lorry-drivers and others who were continually passing on

64

1890

the way to the coast, and the heart of many a " Tommy "
en route for France was gladdened with a tankard of foaming
milk and a Marie biscuit from the hands of old Mother
Bloodworthy, as she was affectionately known in the
neighbourhood. After the war a great change took place.
Her second son, Herbert Bloodworthy, returned home
from the front, where he had served in a mechanized
detachment, determined to put to some use the knowledge
of mechanics he had acquired in the service of his country.
With the money that had been obtained from the sale
of a considerable portion of the farm land to a chemical
syndicate for the erection of a poison-gas factory in 1918,
he decided to build an up-to-date garage. The fifteenth-
century barn at the back of the house proved easily con-
vertible, and all the alteration necessary was to widen
the door and replace the old tiles with corrugated iron.

Herbert's daring and foresight were speedily justified,
and so profitable did the business become that in 1925,
when the old road was widened, straightened and generally

1925

improved, it was decided to expand on a large scale. With the aid of a local firm, Elizabethan Enterprises Ltd., the old house was entirely reconstructed in the Tudor style, seven lock-ups were built, and, with considerable difficulty, a licence obtained. Within a very few months the " Ace of Hearts," as it was now called, was filled to capacity every week-end during the summer, and even in winter did a flourishing trade.

The next few years were ones of increasing prosperity, and when, in 1930, the new Flushbrook by-pass was opened, the vastly increased volume of traffic found ample accommodation in the palatial new premises of the " Hearts are Trumps " roadhouse, for Herbert Bloodworthy had kept abreast of the times and not content with his initial efforts at modernization and enlargement had gone ahead and expanded even further. The garage had been increased in size and could now accommodate over thirty cars at a time and ten new petrol pumps had been installed. The Olde Englishe Grille and the Restaurant

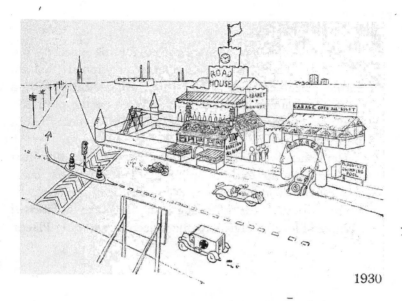

1930

Fleurie catered for all tastes and supplied every species of fresh farm and dairy produce straight from the Argentine, expertly prepared by a large staff of skilled chefs. The American Bar provided light refreshment for those who could not tarry long, and finally in the beautiful new dance hall, with its modernistic sofas, lalique panels and cleverly concealed lighting Ed Sugarprong and his Twenty-Seven White-Hot Tubthumpers provided the hottest jazz to be heard between Hammersmith Broadway and Pelvis Bay. Last year the Pompeian Swimming Pool, complete with artificial waves and floodlit every night from seven till two, was opened with a pretty ceremony in which forty of the loveliest bathing belles in Britain took part.

The fastidious motorist will find at this establishment

67

that everything has been arranged for his especial convenience. There is an excellently equipped first-aid station together with a small operating-theatre with a doctor and nurses in constant attendance on the premises, and next year it is intended to install an up-to-date funeral parlour.

Here then we will take leave of our reader, after first leading him up to the top of the massive tower overlooking the swimming pool, whence we can see far away in the distance the glittering sea, and take a farewell glimpse of lovely Pelvis Bay, the Queen of Watering Places.